Chickens Have Chicks

by Lynn M. Stone

Animals and Their Young

Content Adviser: Terrence E. Young Jr., M.Ed., M.L.S.
Jefferson Parish (La.) Public Schools

Reading Adviser: Dr. Linda D. Labbo,
Department of Reading Education, College of Education,
The University of Georgia

COMPASS POINT BOOKS

Minneapolis, Minnesota

Compass Point Books
3722 West 50th Street, #115
Minneapolis, MN 55410

For more information about Compass Point Books, e-mail your request to:
custserv@compasspointbooks.com

Photographs ©: Lynn M. Stone

Editors: E. Russell Primm and Emily J. Dolbear
Photo Researcher: Svetlana Zhurkina
Photo Selector: Linda S. Koutris
Design: Bradfordesign, Inc.

Library of Congress Cataloging-in-Publication Data

Stone, Lynn M.
    Chickens have chicks / by Lynn M. Stone.
        p. cm. — (Animals and their young)
    Includes bibliographcal references and index.
    Summary: An introduction to the life cycle of chickens from birth to adult, describing their appearance,
feeding habits, growth and more.
    ISBN 0-7565-0000-1 (lib. bdg.)
    1. Chicks—Juvenile literature. [1. Chickens. 2. Animals—Infancy.] I. Title. II. Series: Stone, Lynn M.
Animals and their young.
SF498.4 .S76 2000
636.5'07—dc21   00-008826

Table of Contents

What Are Chicks?

Chicks are baby chickens. A mother chicken is called a **hen**. A father chicken is called a **rooster**.

Chickens may differ from one another in size, color, and even shape. But chickens of all kinds, or breeds, begin life like other birds do—in an egg.

Every egg does not contain an unborn chick. The only eggs that produce chicks are made when a hen and a rooster mate. Those are called fertile eggs because they can produce chicks. The egg you had for breakfast probably was not fertile.

◀ These eggs have chicks inside.

What Does a Hen Do?

Hens lay eggs throughout the year. A nesting hen may lay six to fifteen eggs each time.

After a hen lays a fertile egg, she must keep it warm. The hen will cover the egg with her body for twenty-one days. This is called **incubating**.

Most eggs are taken away from hens, however. The eggs are kept warm in an incubator. An incubator is a tray with electric heat.

◀ A hen sits on her eggs to keep them warm.

How Does a Chick Get Out of the Egg?

Getting out of a tough eggshell is not easy. Each chick has an egg tooth. It is not a real tooth, of course. Birds don't have teeth! An egg tooth is a sharp and hard growth on top of a chick's beak. The chick uses its egg tooth to chip a hole in the shell.

The hole in the shell is called a **pip**. After the chick's work, the egg finally cracks open. Soon after the chick hatches, its egg tooth falls off.

◄ A chick begins to break out of its shell.

What Happens after the Chick Hatches?

When a chicken egg breaks open, a damp little chick crawls out. It is covered with short fluffy feathers called down. The chick is wet from the liquid inside the egg. This liquid is called egg white. It is part of the chick's food in the egg.

◀ Chicks are wet after they crack out of the shell.

What Do Newborn Chicks Look Like?

The chick's feathers dry within a few hours after hatching. Then the down is fluffy.

The chick stays in this cute, downy stage for only about three days. By the fourth day, the chick's longer, stiffer feathers begin to grow. The chick won't really be a good-looking bird again until it's full-grown.

◀ A newborn chick's feathers dry quickly.

What Do Chicks Do?

Like almost all birds, tiny chicks have little or no sense of smell. But they can see, hear, walk, and peep. They also know how to keep warm.

Chicks rely on their feathers to keep warm. But a chick may need more warmth than its down can supply. Chicks often huddle under their mother's wings and feathers. They need their mother's body heat from time to time until they are four to six weeks old. Chicks living away from their mothers keep warm under heating lamps.

◀ A tiny chick makes a peeping noise.

How Do Chicks Feed?

Chicks are able to feed themselves almost as soon as they hatch. The hen doesn't need to bring food to them. When chicks come out of the egg, they are ready to feed themselves.

When chicks hatch, they have the **instinct** to peck with their tiny beaks. They peck at bugs and small seeds.

Chicks follow their mother around. They scratch with the little claws on their toes. They tumble along like a parade of fluffy marshmallows.

◄ Chicks peck for food with their tiny beaks.

What Do Chicks Look Like?

Chicks are much smaller than hens, of course. And chicks don't have as many feathers as adult chickens. It takes twenty to thirty weeks for all their adult feathers to grow in.

Chicks don't have the red, fleshy **combs** and **wattles** we see on adult chickens. The comb grows on the top of a chicken's head. Wattles hang from a chicken's beak.

Adult chickens look very different from chicks.

When Is a Chick Grown Up?

By the time it's an adult, a chick's body has changed greatly. Because it has full wing feathers, a grown-up chick can fly—but not very far. They fly mostly to escape enemies. They also fly to reach perches, where they roost at night.

Being grown up also means that young hens and roosters can have chicks of their own. Some breeds begin laying eggs when they are just three months old. Hens of larger breeds, like giants, are one year old before they have chicks.

◄ A grown-up chick lays her own eggs.

Glossary

comb—the fleshy red growth on top of a chicken's head

hen—a female chicken; a mother chicken

incubating—keeping eggs warm so that they will hatch

instinct—knowing what to do without being taught; a natural behavior

pip—the hole made in an eggshell by the chick inside

rooster—a male chicken; a father chicken

wattle—a fleshy, red body part that hangs from the beak of a chicken

Did You Know?

- In 1990, the United States produced 68 billion chicken eggs.

- Some chickens lay as many as 280 eggs each year.

- Some farms have as many as 1 million chickens.

Want to Know More?

At the Library
Burton, Jane. *Chester the Chick*. New York: Random House, 1988.
Hariton, Anca. *Egg Story*. New York: Dutton Children's Books, 1992.
Legg, Gerald. *From Egg to Chicken*. New York: Franklin Watts, 1998.

On the Web
Kids Farm: Chicks
http://www.kidsfarm.com/chicks.htm
For pictures and captions about chickens and their chicks

Museum of Science and Industry
http://www.msichicago.org/exhibit/chick/chick.html
To watch a chick hatch and to download a movie about chicks

Through the Mail
American Egg Board
1460 Renaissance Drive
Suite 301
Park Ridge, IL 60068
For egg recipes and cooking tips

United Egg Association
1 Massachusetts Avenue, N.W., #800
Washington, DC 20001
For information about the importance of eggs as food

On the Road
Museum of Science and Industry
57th and Lake Shore Drive
Chicago, IL 60601
773/684-1414
800/468-6674 (outside Chicago) To see the chick hatchery exhibit containing
eggs and unborn chicks

Index

About the Author

Lynn M. Stone has written hundreds of children's books and many articles on natural history for various magazines. He has photographed wildlife and domestic animals on all seven continents for such magazines as *National Geographic, Time, Ranger Rick, Natural History, Field and Stream*, and *Audubon*.

Lynn Stone earned a bachelor's degree at Aurora University in Illinois and a master's degree at Northern Illinois University. He taught in the West Aurora schools for several years before becoming a writer-photographer full-time. He lives with his wife and daughter in Batavia, Illinois.